Schaum Fingerpower CHRISTMAS

10 SEASONAL PIANO SOLOS WITH TECHNIQUE WARM-UPS

Arranged by JAMES POTEAT

T0084203

The purpose of Fingerpower Christmas is to provide a seasonal musical experience beyond the traditional **Fingerpower**® series. It offers students a variety of popular Christmas arrangements and are listed in order of difficulty. Technique warm-ups are included for each solo.

CONTENTS

2	**WARM-UPS**
11	**SOLOS**

12	Somewhere in My Memory	24	Christmas Time Is Here
14	Rudolph the Red-Nosed Reindeer	26	Do You Hear What I Hear
16	Here Comes Santa Claus	27	Sleigh Ride
18	The Most Wonderful Time of the Year	28	Winter Wonderland
22	Christmas Island	30	Do You Want to Build a Snowman?

ISBN 978-1-5400-5789-1

Schaum

EXCLUSIVELY DISTRIBUTED BY

HAL•LEONARD®

Visit Hal Leonard Online at
www.halleonard.com

Contact us:
Hal Leonard
7777 West Bluemound Road
Milwaukee, WI 53213
Email: info@halleonard.com

In Europe, contact:
Hal Leonard Europe Limited
42 Wigmore Street
Marylebone, London, W1U 2RN
Email: info@halleonardeurope.com

In Australia, contact:
Hal Leonard Australia Pty. Ltd.
4 Lentara Court
Cheltenham, Victoria, 3192 Australia
Email: info@halleonard.com.au

WARM-UPS

Warm-Up for
"Somewhere in My Memory"
(page 12)

2nds, 3rds & 4ths

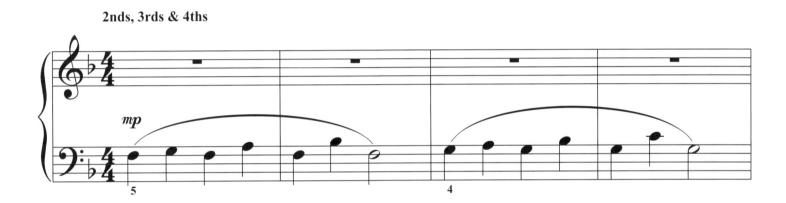

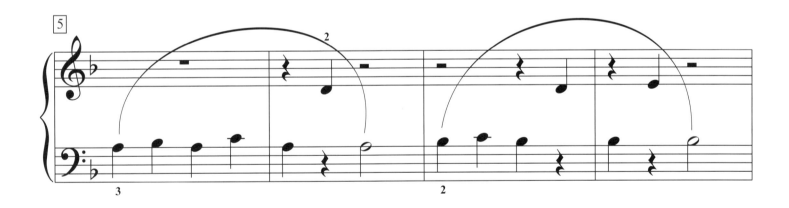

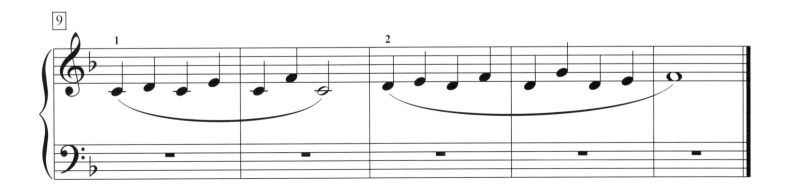

Warm-Ups for
"Rudolph the Red-Nosed Reindeer"
(page 14)

1. TRILLS for the R.H.
Swing the 8th notes.

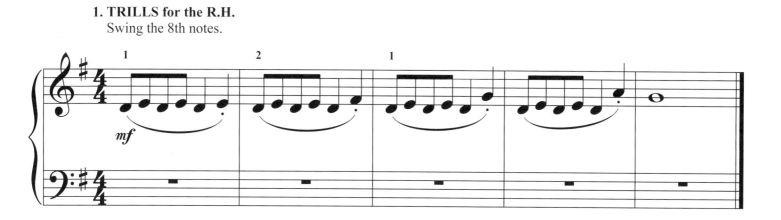

2. SYNCOPATION & ARTICULATION
Swing the 8th notes.

Warm-Ups for
"Here Comes Santa Claus"

(page 16)

1. LEGATO & STACCATO, HANDS TOGETHER

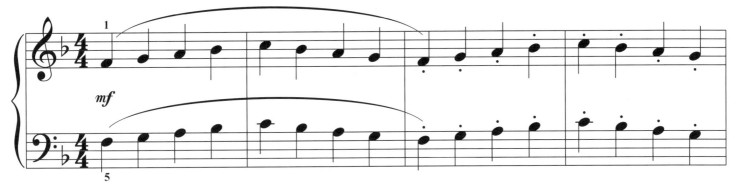

2. SHIFTING with the THUMB, L.H.

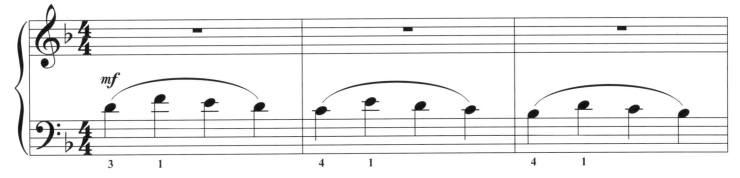

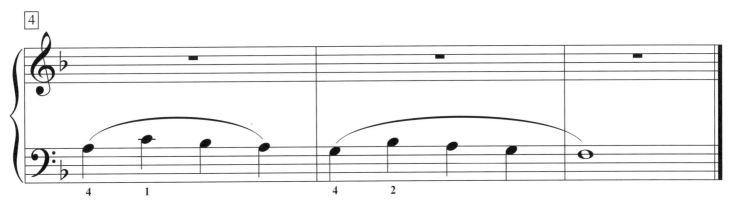

Warm-Up for
"The Most Wonderful Time of the Year"

(page 18)

ARTICULATION
(Staccato and Legato)

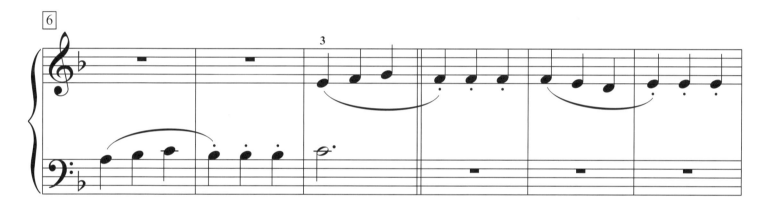

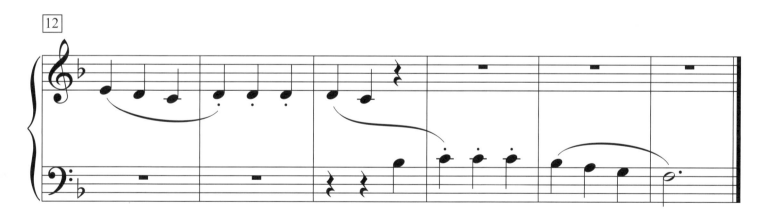

Hint: Before playing the solo on page 18, circle all of the staccatos in the piece.

Warm-Ups for
"Christmas Island"

(page 22)

1. "ISLAND NEIGHBORS" (R.H.)
Swing the 8th notes.

2. 3rds (L.H.)
non-legato

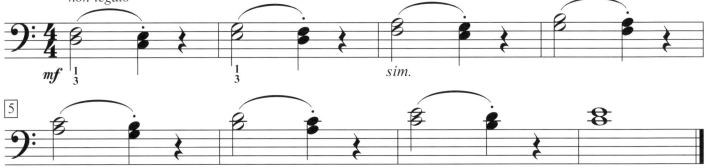

Warm-Up for
"Christmas Time Is Here"

(page 24)

BLOCKED & BROKEN 3rds

Warm-Up for
"Do You Hear What I Hear"
(page 26)

CROSSING THE LEFT HAND
(Tonic & Dominant)

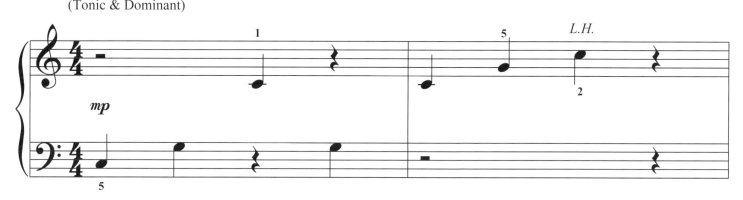

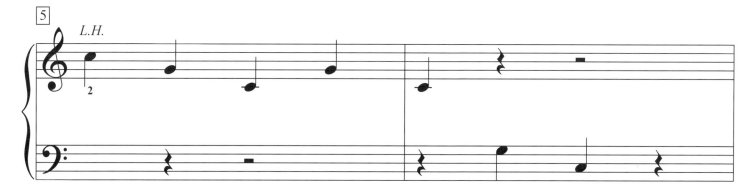

Warm-Ups for
"Sleigh Ride"
(page 27)

1. FOCUS ON WEAKER FINGERS, R.H.

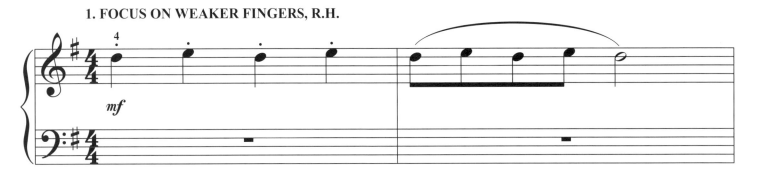

2. CROSS-OVERS with FINGER 2, L.H.

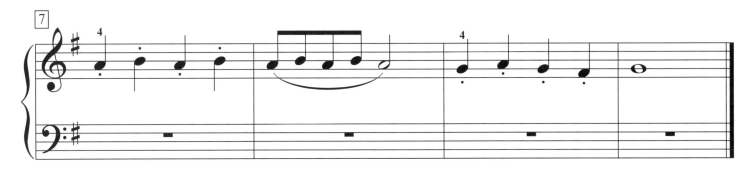

Warm-Ups for
"Winter Wonderland"

(page 28)

1. SWINGING DOWN THE SCALE

Swing the 8th notes.

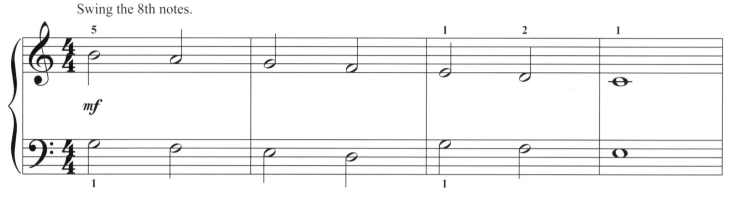

2. "FACE UNAFRAID" LEAPS (R.H.)

Use finger 4 or 5 to make the leaps.

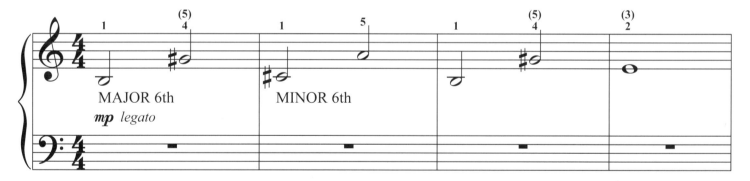

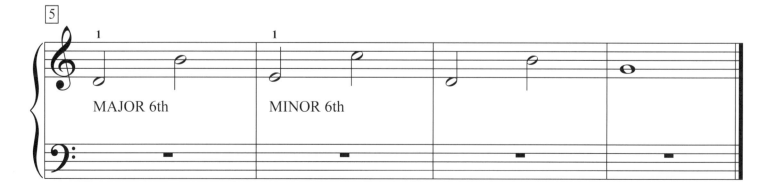

Warm-Ups for
"Do You Want to Build a Snowman?"
(page 30)

1. EXTENDING THE RIGHT HAND

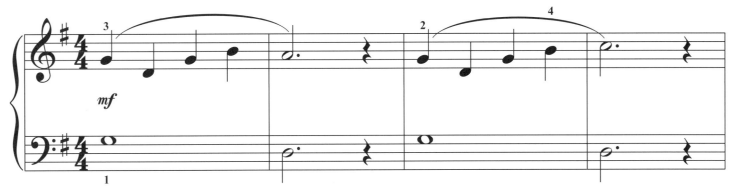

2. SCALE FINALE in LEFT HAND

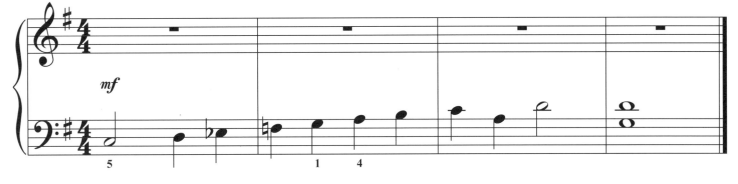

SOLOS

Somewhere in My Memory
from the Twentieth Century Fox Motion Picture HOME ALONE

Words by Leslie Bricusse
Music by John Williams
Arranged by James Poteat

WARM-UP: page 2

Accompaniment (Student plays two octaves higher than written.)

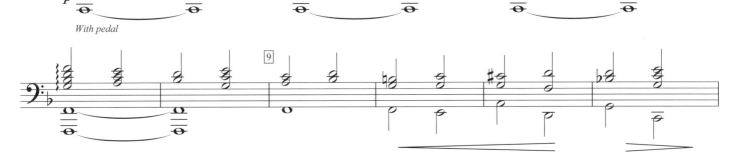

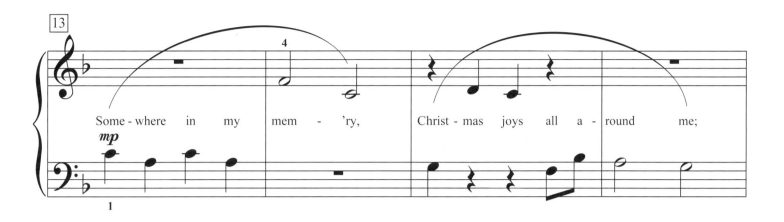

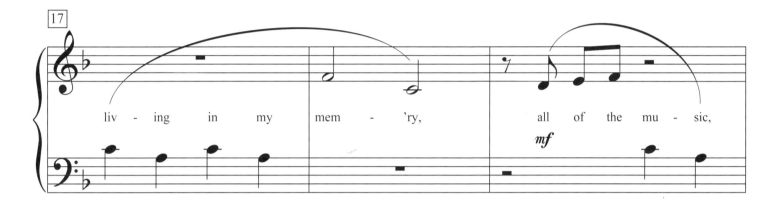

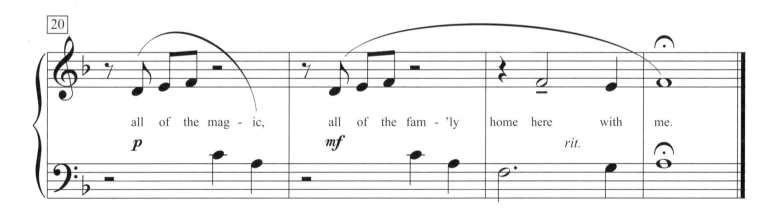

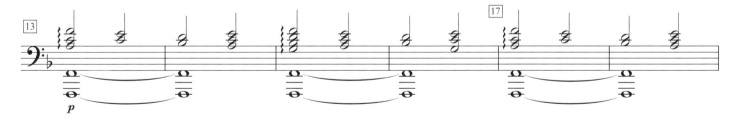

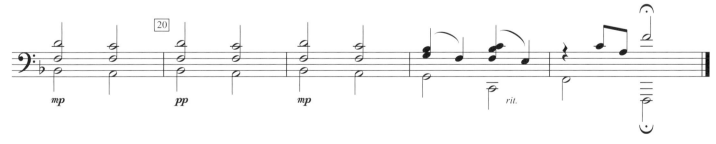

Rudolph the Red-Nosed Reindeer

WARM-UP: page 3

Music and Lyrics by Johnny Marks
Arranged by James Poteat

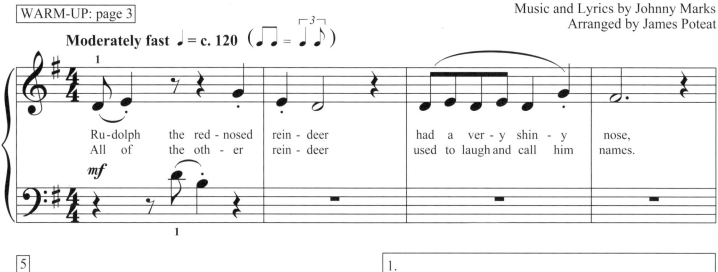

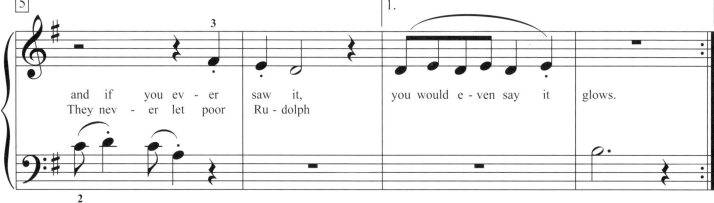

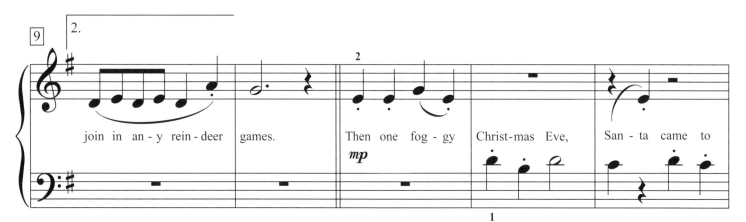

Accompaniment (Student plays one octave higher than written.)

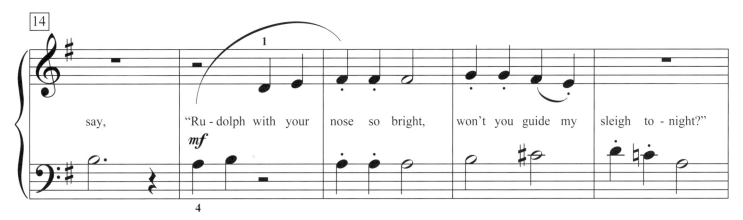

say, "Ru - dolph with your nose so bright, won't you guide my sleigh to - night?"

Then how the rein - deer loved him, as they shout - ed out with glee:

"Ru - dolph the red - nosed rein - deer, you'll go down in his - to - ry!"

Here Comes Santa Claus
(Right Down Santa Claus Lane)

Words and Music by Gene Autry
and Oakley Haldeman
Arranged by James Poteat

WARM-UP: page 4

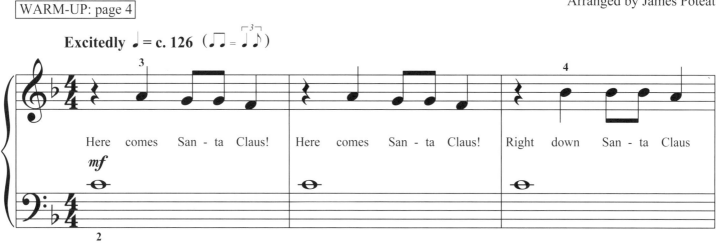

Accompaniment (Student plays one octave higher than written.)

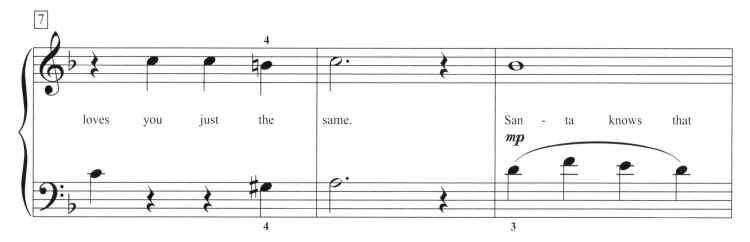

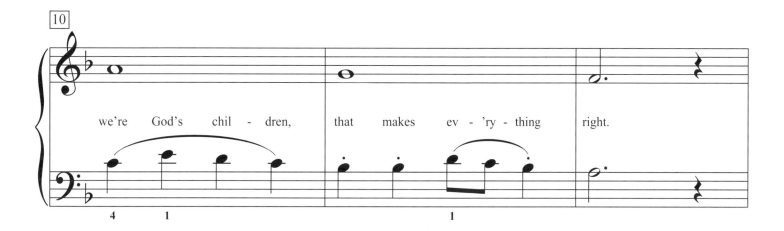

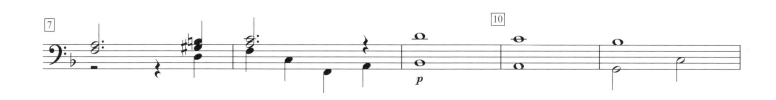

The Most Wonderful Time of the Year

Words and Music by Eddie Pola
and George Wyle
Arranged by James Poteat

WARM-UP: page 5

Carefree ♩ = c. 148   Play *legato* except where marked.

Accompaniment (Student plays one octave higher than written.)

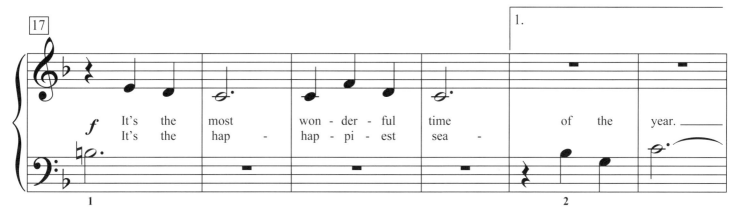

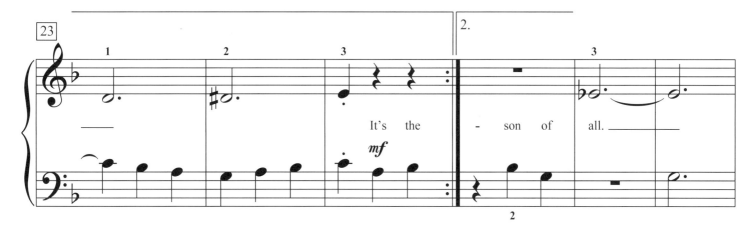

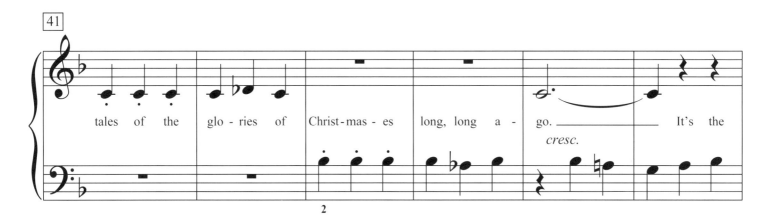

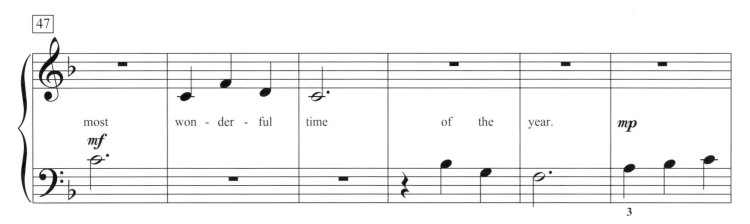

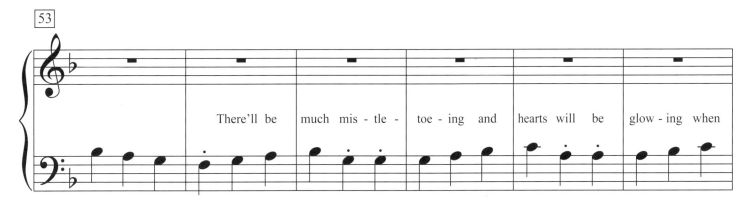

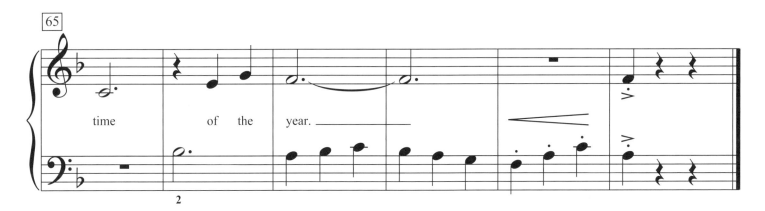

Christmas Island

WARM-UP: page 6

Words and Music by Lyle Moraine
Arranged by James Poteat

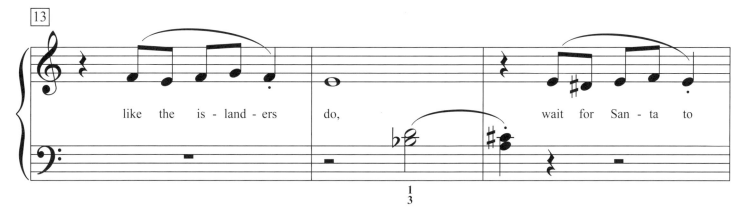

like the is - land - ers do, wait for San - ta to

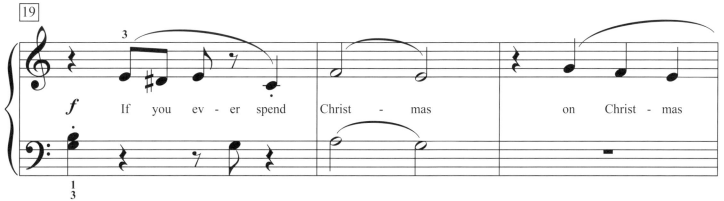

sail in with your pres - ents in a ca - noe?

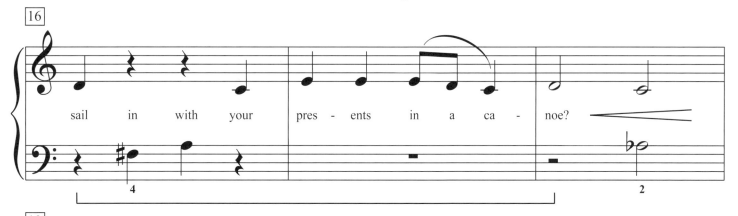

If you ev - er spend Christ - mas on Christ - mas

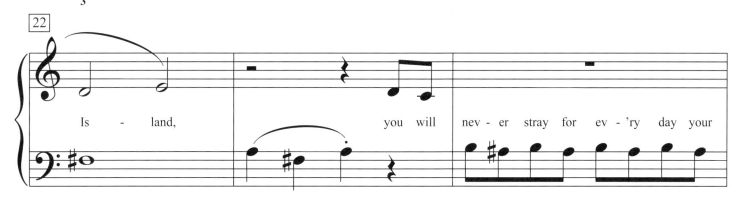

Is - land, you will nev - er stray for ev - 'ry day your

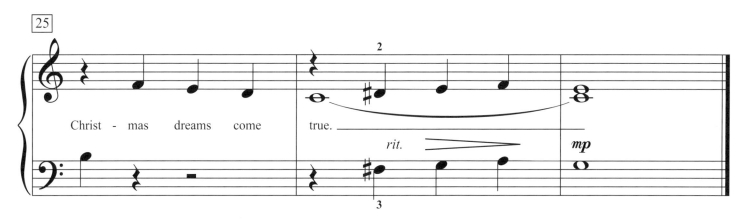

Christ - mas dreams come true. _____
rit. *mp*

Christmas Time Is Here
from A CHARLIE BROWN CHRISTMAS

Words by Lee Mendelson
Music by Vince Guaraldi

WARM-UP: page 6

Slowly ♩ = c. 76

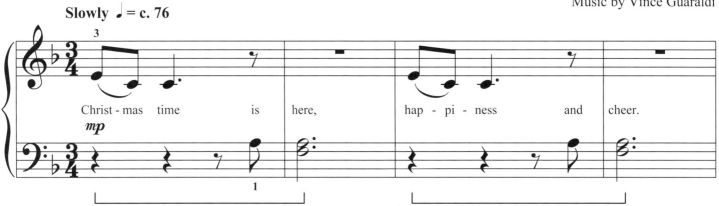

Christ - mas time is here, hap - pi - ness and cheer.

Fun for all that chil - dren call their fa - v'rite time of year.

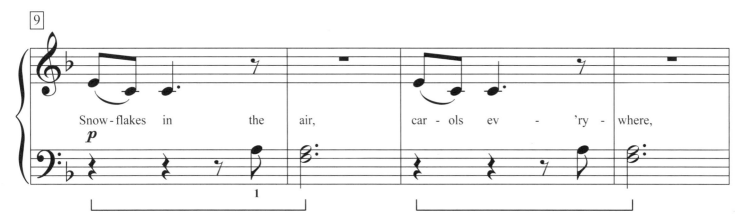

Snow - flakes in the air, car - ols ev - 'ry - where,

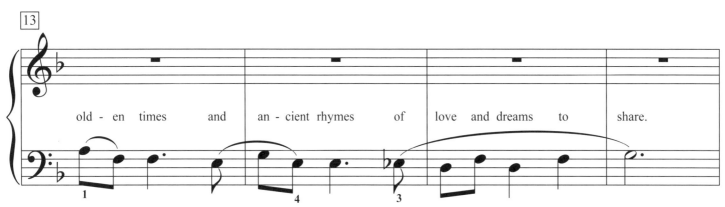

old - en times and an - cient rhymes of love and dreams to share.

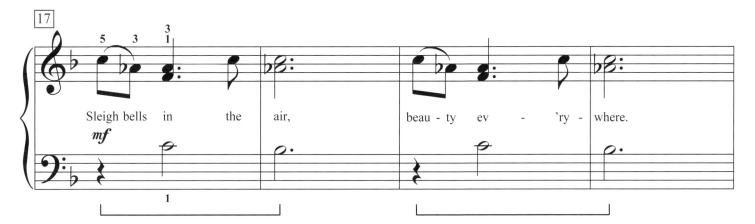

Sleigh bells in the air, beau - ty ev - 'ry - where.

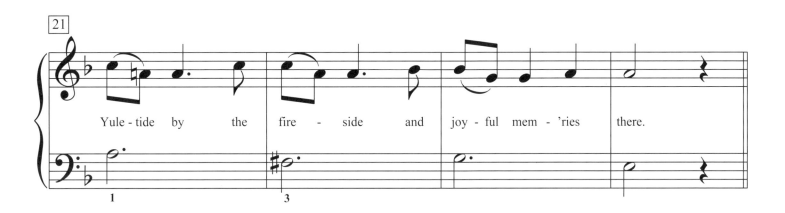

Yule - tide by the fire - side and joy - ful mem - 'ries there.

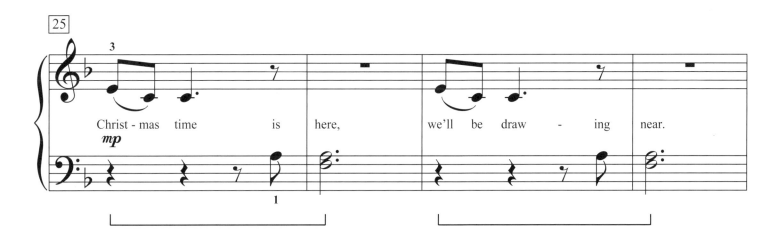

Christ - mas time is here, we'll be draw - ing near.

Oh, that we could al - ways see such spir - it through the year.

Do You Hear What I Hear

Words and Music by Noel Regney
and Gloria Shayne
Arranged by James Poteat

WARM-UP: page 7

Steadily forward ♩ = c. 88

Sleigh Ride

Music by Leroy Anderson
Arranged by James Poteat

WARM-UP: page 8

With energy ♩ = c. 138

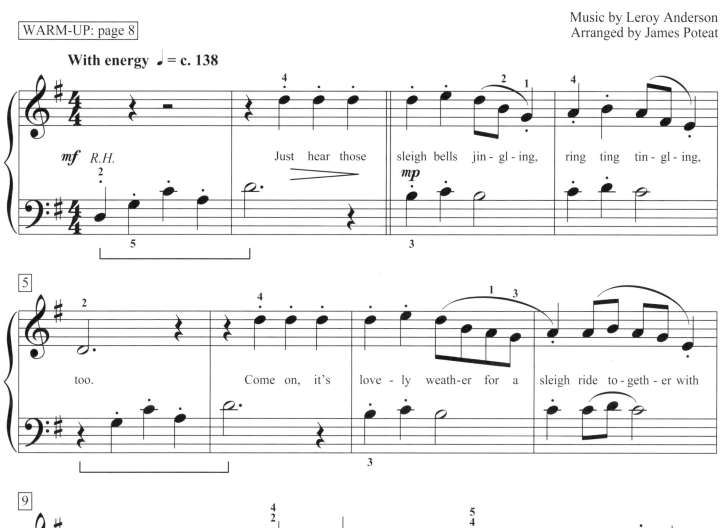

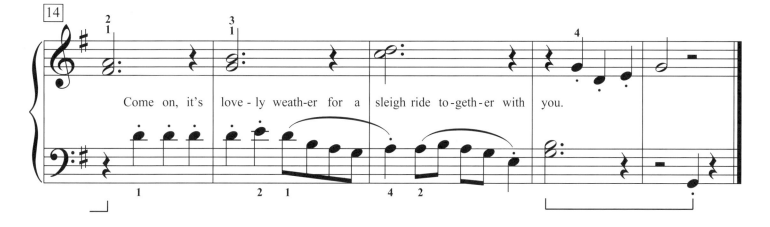

Winter Wonderland

Words by Dick Smith
Music by Felix Bernard
Arranged by James Poteat

WARM-UP: page 9

Moderate Swing ♩ = c. 120

He'll say, "Are you mar-ried." We'll say, "No, man, but you can do the job when you're in

town!" Lat - er on we'll con - spi - re as we

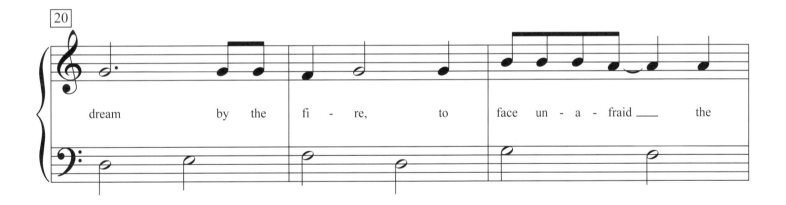

dream by the fi - re, to face un - a - fraid ___ the

plans that we've made, ___ walk - in' in a win - ter won - der - land.

Do You Want to Build a Snowman?

from FROZEN

Music and Lyrics by Kristen Anderson-Lopez
and Robert Lopez
Arranged by James Poteat

WARM-UP: page 10

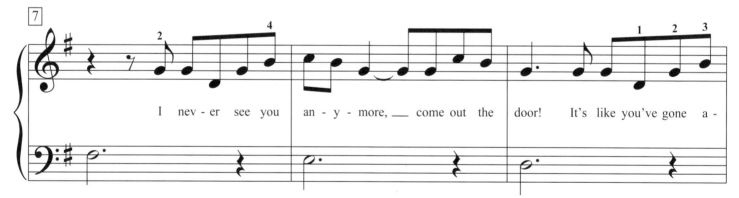

now we're not. _____ I wish you could tell me why.

Do you want to build a snow-man? It does-n't have to be a

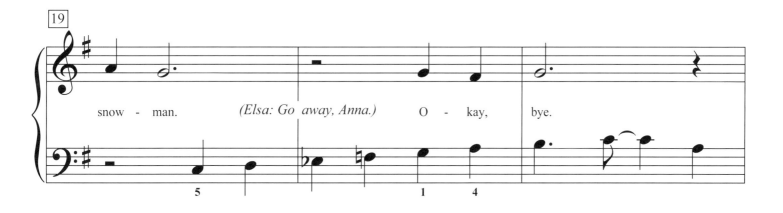

snow - man. *(Elsa: Go away, Anna.)* O - kay, bye.

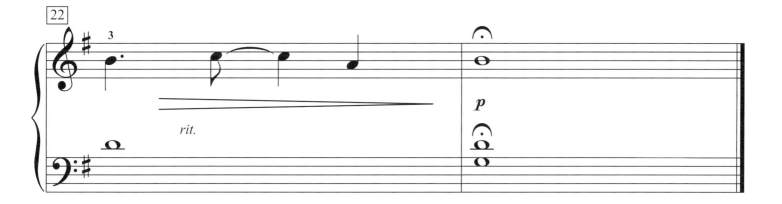

ABOUT THE ARRANGER

Since 2007 **James Poteat** has taught piano, trombone, euphonium, music theory, and composition in Woodstock, Georgia. Mr. Poteat works with students of all ages and skill levels and is equally comfortable in the worlds of popular and classical music. James is constantly arranging music for his students and is dedicated to creating and using materials of the highest quality. Learn more about James and his work by visiting **www.musicalintentions.com**.